Happy hu,

TAMPA BAY
Scavenger

Joshua Ginsberg

Reedy Press
PO Box 5131
St. Louis, MO 63139, USA
www.reedypress.com

Library of Congress Control Number: 2021935247

ISBN: 9781681063454

Cover and interior design by Claire Ford

Cover and interior photos by Joshua Ginsberg

Printed in the United States of America
21 22 23 24 25   5 4 3 2 1

Dedication

For all of the weirdos and RPG players,
Exploring their dungeons, crypts, and lairs
For those who spend time doing what they love best
Especially when it involves a quest,
You seekers of secrets and history,
Attuned to magic and mystery,
Who wander far more for wisdom and wonder
Than ever you do for riches to plunder,
For all who wish such a treasure to find,
For your pleasure have I this adventure designed.

Contents

Acknowledgments...v

Introduction vi

Map...viii

Hillsborough County.................................... 2

Downtown Tampa..2

Ybor City 22

University of Tampa Area........................32

Hyde Park Area 36

South Tampa... 42

Northwest Tampa 50

Tampa Heights 56

Greater Carrollwood and
Forest Hills..60

Sulphur Springs, Seminole Heights,
and Lowry Park 64

Temple Terrace and
Uptown Tampa...................................... 70

Plant City...74

Pinellas County 78

Central Arts, Waterfront, and
Edge Districts... 78

St. Petersburg: Downtown and
the Pier.. 86

Historic Old Northeast and
Historic Uptown................................... 94

St. Petersburg: Grand Central
District, Historic Kenwood,
Warehouse Arts District,
and Jordan Park.................................... 98

Gulfport, Jungle Terrace, and
Azalea Homes..................................... 104

St. Pete Beach and Pass-A-Grille
Beach.. 108

Indian Rocks Beach and
Treasure Island....................................112

Largo and Belleair 120

Clearwater and Clearwater Beach.......124

Dunedin 134

Tarpon Springs...138

Safety Harbor and Oldsmar 144

Palm Harbor..150

Manatee and Sarasota Counties.................. 152

Bradenton 152

Palma Sola, Cortez, and
Anna Maria Island 158

Indian Beach, Sapphire Shores,
and North Trail.................................... 164

Downtown Sarasota, Gillespie Park,
Rosemary District, and Park East ... 170

St. Armands, Lido Key,
Longboat Key, and City Island.......180

Acknowledgments

The list of those who deserve recognition far exceeds what space I have here. Topping that list however, are Josh Stevens, Barbara Northcott, and everyone at Reedy Press, not only for seeing the greater potential in a dozen riddles I had created, but also for their guidance, patience, and support.

This work benefited from the input of Tiffany Razzano (Wordier Than Thou), Alex and Trudy at the Clearwater Historical Society Museum and Cultural Center, and staff members at Sunken Gardens and St. Pete Store & Visitor Center. I received invaluable advice from fellow authors Dea Hoover and Jenna Kashou. Thank you also to The Paperback Exchange Bookstore, South Tampa Trading Co., Grindhaus Brew Lab, and the Museum of Motherhood for ongoing support and friendship. I also made frequent use of *Atlas Obscura*, *Roadside America* and *Abandoned Florida*.

I could not have completed this book without friends and family including Andy and Bob, Howard and Debbie, David and Myrna, Ali, Jeremy and the boys, Barbara and Jon, Candi and Tom, Jason Ewing, Larry Hayward, Mary Dismore, Bobby Conway, Andrew Tschudy, Gary Silber, Alec Bruggenthies, Theo Menard, Ben Workman, Jon/Jeff/Jenna, Ayesha Hamid, Pirates of Maddness, theStudio at GT, Masterminds Tampa Bay, and many others.

Above all, thanks and many shopping days are owed to my wife, Jen, for her love and willingness to schlep to strange places with me, and to our loyal companion, Tinker Bell.

Lastly, thank you to all of those who shaped my world into a more fascinating and inspired place to be, from Gary Gygax to Forrest Fenn, J. R. R. Tolkien, Misha Collins, Ernest Cline, Anthony Bourdain, and Robert Ripley.

Introduction

Mazes, puzzles, riddles, and quests filled my childhood world. I remember spending days at a time solving complex mazes, and then eventually creating my own, filling page after page of graph paper with elaborate designs and sharing them with like-minded friends. We spent countless hours watching movies about treasure hunts like *The Goonies* and trying to solve and create J. R. R. Tolkien-styled riddles. At some point, all of those activities were boxed up, labeled "childhood stuff," and carted off to an attic or garage somewhere in my mind palace. They probably would have stayed there, hidden away and forgotten, if not for a series of events that put me on a path to rediscovering that sense of wonder I experienced as a kid, that same path that resulted in my writing *Secret Tampa Bay: A Guide to the Weird, Wonderful, and Obscure.*

This has led me back to riddles and scavenger hunts. For one thing, over the last five years I've participated regularly in something called the Greatest International Scavenger Hunt, (GISH) devised by actor Misha Collins. Jen and I also create and work our way through various adventure lists—both locally and when we travel. These incorporate unique museums, stores, ghost tours, and any sort of scavenger hunt activities we can find-from the Urban Bourbon Passport in Louisville to a stamp book of the various botanical gardens throughout Philadelphia to the Gulp Coast and Ale Trail here at home. All of these are fun and memorable means of collecting experiences and interacting with places in a new and novel manner.

Which brings me to the book you are now holding. It dawned on me that if I, and apparently many others, seem to enjoy unlocking clues that lead to various historical sites and natural wonders, rather than just participating in such activities, why not try my hand at creating one? I quickly jotted down a couple dozen riddles, and shared those with the folks at Reedy Press, who not only appreciated the idea, but asked if I could come up with enough of them to fill an entire book. Never one to shy away from a creative challenge, I set about architecting *Tampa Bay Scavenger*—drawing on the research I'd already done for *Secret Tampa Bay* as well as the work I was doing for an upcoming book, *Oldest Tampa Bay*, and added to those a great many other sites that hadn't made their way into either book, but still deserved recognition. As things began to open back up after the pandemic, I refined and tested my riddles. The final product is, I believe, the most elaborate scavenger hunt ever devised within the Tampa Bay area.

There isn't technically a right or wrong way to use a book like this, but if you plan to partake in the hunt as I have planned it, please visit the website at www.tbscavenger.com. Ultimately, however you choose to utilize *Tampa Bay Scavenger*, whether you are a visitor or lifelong resident of the area looking for a weekend family activity, a teacher seeking something clever to incorporate into a local history lesson plan, or a devoted local explorer, I hope that it will bring you fun, a bit of challenge, and maybe ever so slightly alter your perspective just enough to reveal the secret face of the Tampa Bay area.

Hillsborough County

1 Downtown Tampa
2 Ybor City
3 University of Tampa Area
4 Hyde Park Area
5 South Tampa
6 Northwest Tampa
7 Tampa Heights
8 Greater Carrollwood
9 Forest Hills
10 Sulphur Springs
11 Seminole Heights
12 Lowry Park
13 Temple Terrace
14 Uptown Tampa
15 Plant City

Pinellas County

1 Central Arts District
2 Waterfront District
3 Edge District
4 Downtown St. Petersburg
5 St. Pete Pier
6 Historic Old Northeast St. Petersburg
7 Historic Uptown St. Petersburg
8 Grand Central Historic District
9 Historic Kenwood
10 Warehouse Arts District
11 Jordan Park
12 Gulfport
13 Jungle Terrace
14 Azalea Homes
15 St. Pete Beach
16 Pass-a-Grille Beach
17 Indian Rocks Beach
18 Treasure Island
19 Largo
20 Belleair
21 Clearwater
22 Clearwater Beach
23 Dunedin
24 Tarpon Springs
25 Safety Harbor
26 Oldsmar
27 Palm Harbor

Manatee and Sarasota Counties

1 Bradenton
2 Palma Sola
3 Cortez
4 Anna Maria Island
5 Indian Beach
6 Sapphire Shores
7 North Trail
8 Downtown Sarasota
9 Gillespie Park
10 Rosemary District
11 Park East
12 St. Armands
13 Lido Key
14 Longboat Key
15 City Island

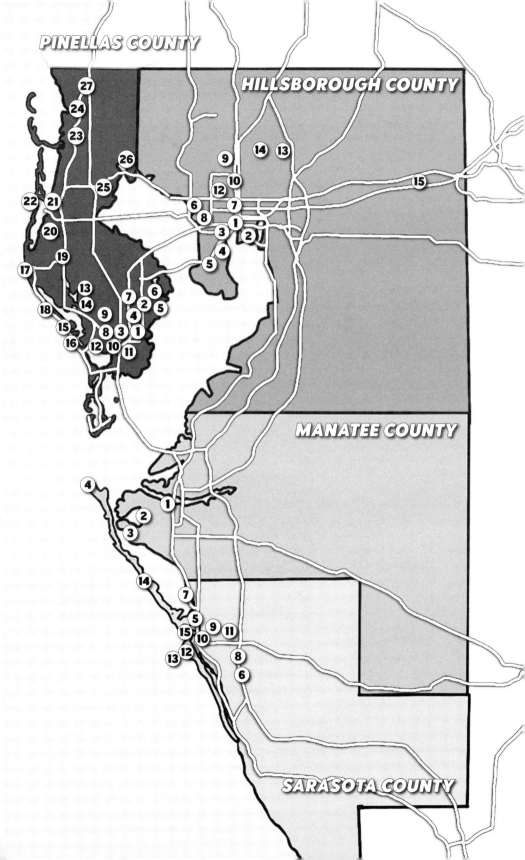

PINELLAS COUNTY

HILLSBOROUGH COUNTY

MANATEE COUNTY

SARASOTA COUNTY

Hillsborough County

Established in 1834, Hillsborough County is home to the city of Tampa (the third-largest in Florida by population). The city and surrounding areas grew from the military stronghold Fort Brooke, which was central to the Seminole Wars. Henry Plant brought the railroad to town, Vicente Martinez Ybor built his own cigar factory town (giving the city the moniker "Cigar City"), and more recently the Lightning and the Buccaneers have won their respective championships.

1

Many fortunes in Tampa
In time were made and lost,
One is here remembered
On a bridge you've likely crossed.

2

Lennon's forever in the weeds
Whether it's early or late.
But why he's alone outside the hotel
Is a subject still up for debate.

3

"Pretty as a postcard":
That's what many visitors see,
Now locate the iconic mural
That takes the phrase literally.

4

At this corner a young preacher
To the downtrodden would impart
Wisdom and verse from the Bible;
It's where he got his start.

5

Curled up on a bench in front of the church,
This sculpture has left some offended.
More likely, discussion of homelessness
Is what the artist intended.

6

Once the tallest building in town
Until the Sapphire lost its gleam.
Recently given the title of "palace,"
Former glory it hopes to redeem.

_____

_____

7

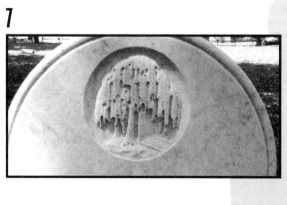

The Ashleys are not today parted;
As spouses together they lay.
No longer the secret it once was
That they chose to live that way.

_____

_____

8

At the park that bears his name,
A figure of wisdom and insights.
Many the contributions he made
As an advocate for civil rights.

9

This museum tells the stories
Of those who respond to a blaze;
Horse-drawn equipment and specialized gear
Just a fraction of what it displays.

10

This object outside the station
Makes time no mystery.
The clock reveals the hour,
The base records history.

_____

_____

11

Truth and Justice is her name,
No foolishness will she abide.
In green and gold, her message bold
She's dignity personified.

_____

_____

12

Within the spherical sculpture
A figure, arms raised toward the skies
Celebrating his freedom
From the name of the piece we surmise.

13

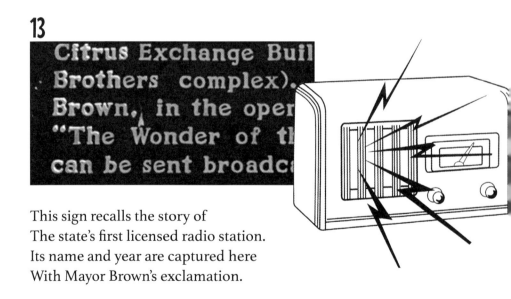

Citrus Exchange Buil
Brothers complex).
Brown, in the oper
"The Wonder of tl
can be sent broadca

This sign recalls the story of
The state's first licensed radio station.
Its name and year are captured here
With Mayor Brown's exclamation.

14

The oldest of its kind in town
(for liquor, that is, not beers),
It's been the center of the wheel
For over 70 years.

15

Fink still works the projector,
At least that's what some say.
He smokes as he drifts through the aisles
In Eberson's palace to stay.

16

Once flanked by Woolworth and Newberry,
This building with a bronze marquee
And terra-cotta work on both facades
Was the vision of G. E. Mackey.

_____

_____

17

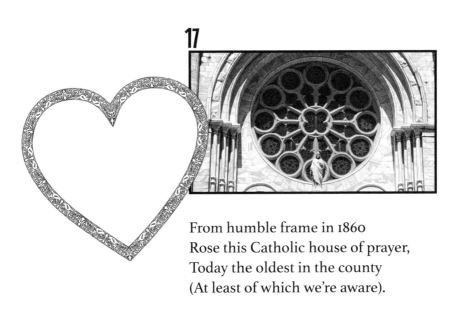

From humble frame in 1860
Rose this Catholic house of prayer,
Today the oldest in the county
(At least of which we're aware).

_____

_____

18

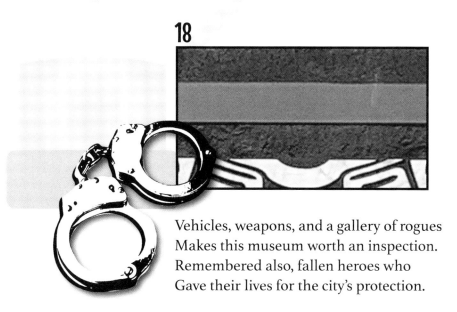

Vehicles, weapons, and a gallery of rogues
Makes this museum worth an inspection.
Remembered also, fallen heroes who
Gave their lives for the city's protection.

19

Mary no longer sells her fruit
From her downtown Tampa stall,
But even today she's remembered in stone
Where once stood an outdoor mall.

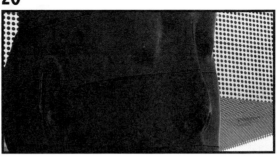

Laura's in front of the museum,
Her hair tied back in a bun.
Her eyes are closed, she looks within
While her iron skin soaks up the sun.

At the age of 27,
Death silenced Jimi's guitar.
Find near the old Curtis Hixon Hall
A tribute to this fallen star.

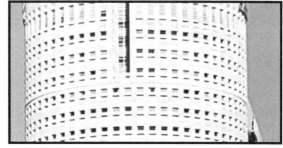

Uniquely cylindrical is my design,
Amongst my peers, a point of pride.
A beauty, a beer can, both I've been called,
But that's not for me to decide.

23

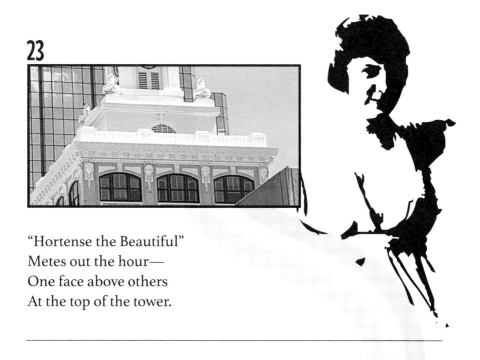

"Hortense the Beautiful"
Metes out the hour—
One face above others
At the top of the tower.

24

There's a story that's told in images bold
Of a city alongside the bay.
Today, from where it hangs on the wall,
It reveals more than words can say.

_____

_____

25

Tampa's first paved sidewalk
Was of marble, not concrete.
Archie placed it around his building;
A patch is preserved near the street.

_____

_____

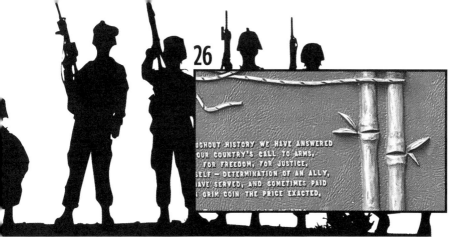

26

Of those sent abroad, our country to serve,
Some do not come back.
Missing or captured, their fates unknown,
But memorialized on this plaque.

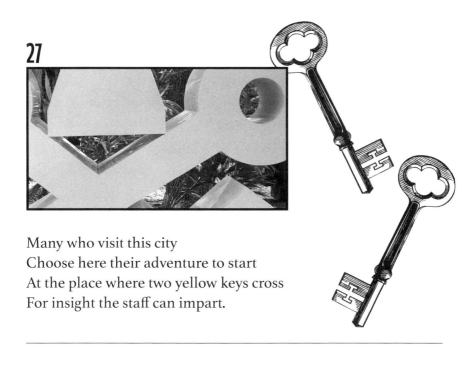

27

Many who visit this city
Choose here their adventure to start
At the place where two yellow keys cross
For insight the staff can impart.

28

To raise funds for roads and highways
Sixteen cars from this point departed
On a four-day round trip to Jacksonville:
Thus the great auto race started.

_____

_____

29

The Buccaneer's very first draft pick
Wears his number, 63,
Immortalized less for his role on the field
Than in the community.

_____

_____

30

Blue is the Truist color in
The city skyline at night.
It's a tower of finance you now seek,
Crowned with a pyramid of light.

31

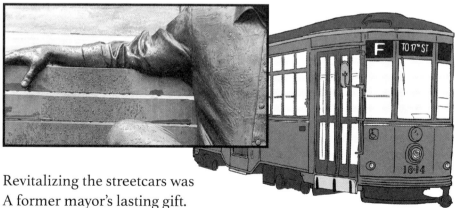

Revitalizing the streetcars was
A former mayor's lasting gift.
You can sit on the bench here beside him
To say thanks while you wait for a lift.

32

The man who helped conjure the Lightning
Is holding his own stick of fire.
On his fingers, the rings of a player,
Though his clothing is business attire.

33

Along the river you'll find this bust,
A tribute to the builders of mounds.
Here they worked and lived their lives
Before there were roads and towns.

34

Find this maritime memorial mural:
The Tampa crew's fate it denotes,
When in 1918 all hands were lost,
A victim of German U-boats.

_____

_____

35

A space for reflection by the river,
A cenotaph where once stood a fort.
Under stylized metal, cypress branches
Through Tampa's past and present sort.

_____

_____

36

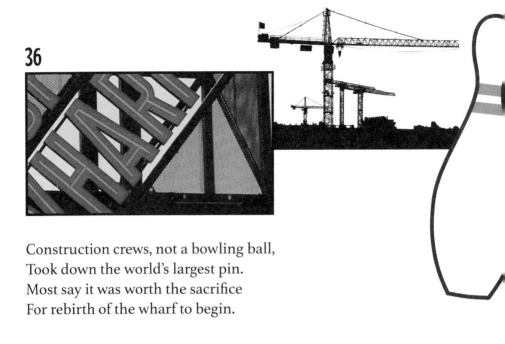

Construction crews, not a bowling ball,
Took down the world's largest pin.
Most say it was worth the sacrifice
For rebirth of the wharf to begin.

37

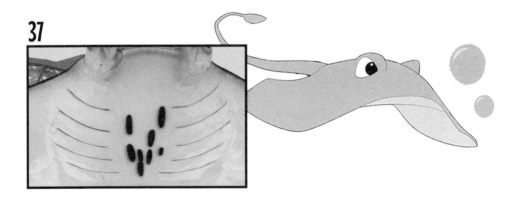

One might assume this manta ray
Has escaped the aquarium's tanks.
But for the photo op and the shade
It provides, many folks give thanks.

38

This 19-ton abstract landmark
Some viewers refuse to call art.
And it's hard to deny that the casual eye
Sees a bird that is bursting apart.

39

When I was first assembled for war
More than 500 numbered my class.
Now I'm one of just four, a museum my core,
My crew volunteers, not brass.

1

The heart of this old factory,
A meticulous ticking machine.
They gave it the title "El Reloj";
Today it can still be seen.

2

Solemn stands this sheriff,
In the shadow a flag has cast.
He guards the fallen heroes
To ensure their memories last.

3

The words of a Cuban hero
Brought the workers' blood to a boil.
Find the park where his likeness stands
Atop his native soil.

4

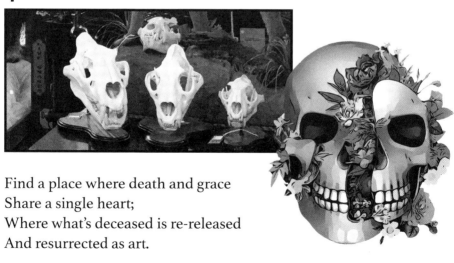

Find a place where death and grace
Share a single heart;
Where what's deceased is re-released
And resurrected as art.

5

ITO TRAFFICANT

Despite his name
No saint was he.
Find where this boss
Rests peacefully.

_____

_____

6

Roland is leaning against a brick wall,
A newspaper in his hand.
Of local machinations he wrote
So his readers could understand.

_____

_____

7

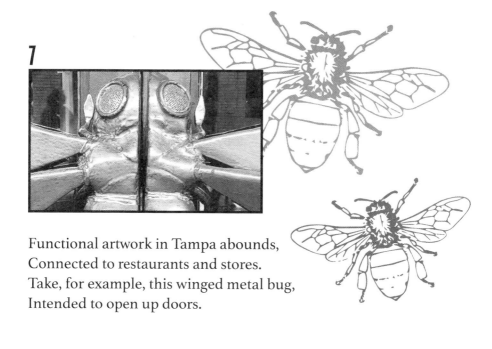

Functional artwork in Tampa abounds,
Connected to restaurants and stores.
Take, for example, this winged metal bug,
Intended to open up doors.

8

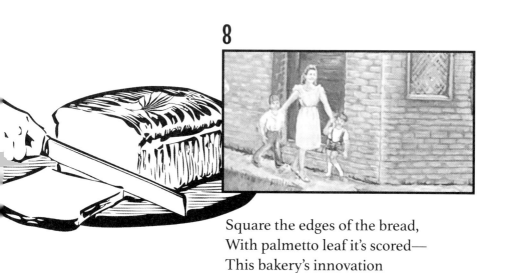

Square the edges of the bread,
With palmetto leaf it's scored—
This bakery's innovation
Makes the local cuisine most adored.

9

Three bent legs, three ears of wheat
And the head of a monster from myth;
The triskelion symbol you'll find at a place
To support those who brought it with.

10

Music, freedom, and craft beers
Keep company behind the bar
Over which an iconic lady
Is smashing her fine guitar.

11

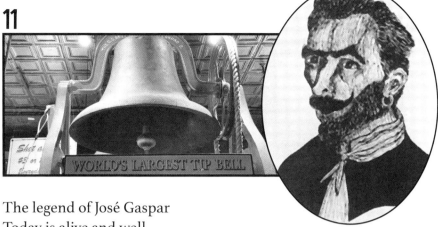

The legend of José Gaspar
Today is alive and well.
Behind the bar in his Grotto
You'll find this gigantic bell.

12

Forever in Ybor arriving
Is this immigrant family of four,
Reminder of those early settlers
Departing from some distant shore.

13

More likely you'll find here a Guinness
Than discussion of *Finnegan's Wake*.
There's bangers and mash on the menu
At this beloved Irish author's namesake.

14

Salads and drinks made table-side
And flamenco shows at night
In this, the oldest restaurant in town,
That gives the Gonzmarts their might.

15

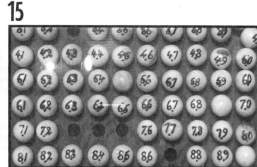

Bolita was a popular game of chance
That brought to town organized crime.
You'll find today the last known board,
Preserved under glass for all time.

16

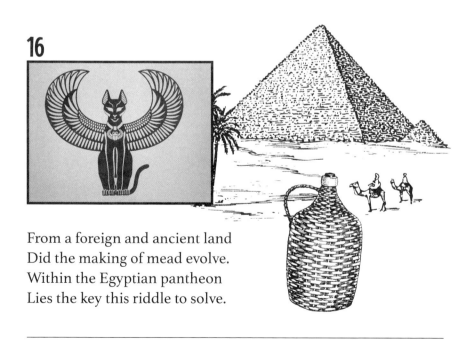

From a foreign and ancient land
Did the making of mead evolve.
Within the Egyptian pantheon
Lies the key this riddle to solve.

17

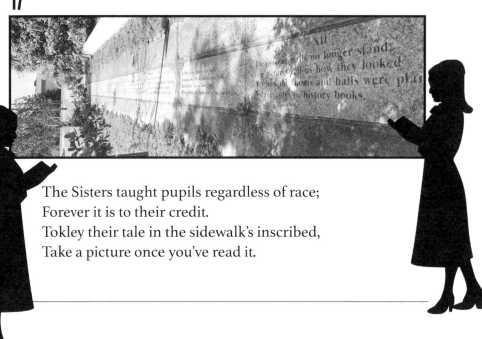

The Sisters taught pupils regardless of race;
Forever it is to their credit.
Tokley their tale in the sidewalk's inscribed,
Take a picture once you've read it.

18

Built in 1886
And called then the Cherokee Club,
Where Roosevelt, Churchill and Cleveland stayed
Before it was a restaurant and pub.

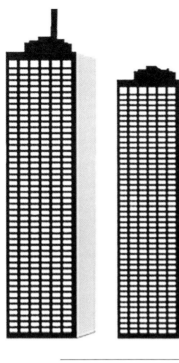

19

Silver figures race to assist
Those under the broken tower.
Shining heroes are they indeed,
Compassion their strength and power.

20

A talented artist
Too soon made late,
Remembered in a mural
He helped to create.

1

There aren't so many parks in town
Where one can expect to find Snow,
Save for the smallest of them all—
The place you must now go.

_____

_____

2

Tribute to a president
You'll find in front of Plant's palace.
Tampa was his penultimate stop
Before the ill-fated trip to Dallas.

_____

_____

3

Once the jewel in Henry's crown,
Now a university and museum;
But in the first room past the entranceway,
On the wall you still can see him.

4

The placement of this cannon
Might strike some folks as strange.
Prepared, it seems, to defend the school
Against the Oxford Exchange.

5

Forces of nature are all well and good
Till they part you from family and friends.
Defeating this one that Babson most hated
On our effort now depends.

_____

_____

6

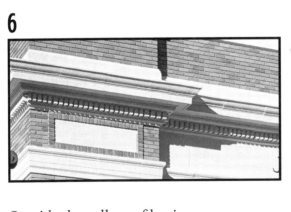

Outside the college of business
A marker proclaims to all
How 587 feet
Once flew this slugger's ball.

_____

_____

7

When we talk about Greeks on campus
Most picture parties and beer,
Not this one at the athletic center
Who's practicing throwing a spear.

8

May those who enter
grow in their faith and life's value
and build a better world for all.

This small Zen garden on campus
For students should suffice
To find a moment of inner peace
And heed Mr. Sykes' advice.

1

If author Alec had stayed in London
His home would have been a flat.
Instead, it's a bungalow on this path
Where he chose to hang his hat.

2

A hidden spot, where you could be free
From Volstead's watchful eye.
But you'll need to know the secret code
Unless you would rather stay dry.

Behind the somewhat bland façade
Hides a wine cellar beyond compare
Be sure to ask your server for
The tour that's offered there.

In their median pasture
Graze three forms equine.
Beneath the sun, as cars speed past,
See how their metal hides shine.

5

From underneath the Wallace Yew
To a monument by the bay,
This rock from a Scottish hero's home
Has traveled a very long way.

6

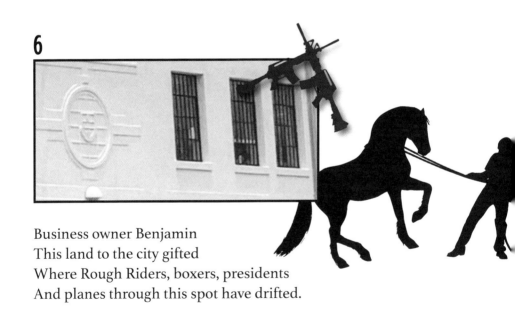

Business owner Benjamin
This land to the city gifted
Where Rough Riders, boxers, presidents
And planes through this spot have drifted.

7

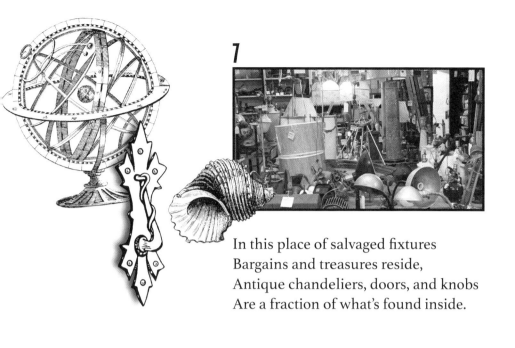

In this place of salvaged fixtures
Bargains and treasures reside,
Antique chandeliers, doors, and knobs
Are a fraction of what's found inside.

8

No soldiers bound for Cuba today
Will you find here prepared to embark;
Just this marker to let you know
That their camp is now a park.

9

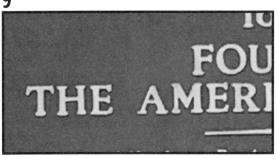 

Educator, nurse, and Red Cross founder,
Clara's recognized at this location
For supporting civilians and troops alike
As a true pioneer in her vocation.

_____

_____

10

It's seldom you see a home such as this
Where Queen Anne and colonial styles revive.
For 120 years it has stood
Just a short walk from Bayshore Drive.

_____

_____

11

Find this tribute to Jannus,
His famous flight here recalled.
Etched in stone, atop of which
An airplane propeller's installed.

12

Past four lions at the fountain
In a circle ringed with trees,
There, from an artist's structure,
Hangs no lock but many keys.

1

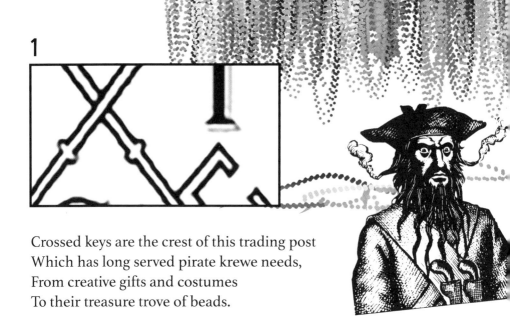

Crossed keys are the crest of this trading post
Which has long served pirate krewe needs,
From creative gifts and costumes
To their treasure trove of beads.

_____

_____

2

They say this hotel bar was once
A place for those of ill repute
To have a drink and an alibi
That no one would dare refute.

_____

_____

3

This marker pays tribute to Bellamy,
Though few recognize his name;
But everyone knows the pledge he penned
That's achieved enduring fame.

_____

_____

4

From her rooftop perch she guards
The antiques and treasures below,
And when the sunlight strikes her right,
It sets her scales aglow.

_____

_____

5

This place was once a trolley stop,
Later known as Jules Verne Park.
Today it sports a different name
And a pier from which pirates embark.

6

On one day each year
This beam from the towers
Measures in shadow
The tragic hours.

7

Ionic pilasters and terra-cotta tile
Make this building a rarity.
Behind its bronze doors and up two floors
Is a room for reading the sea.

8

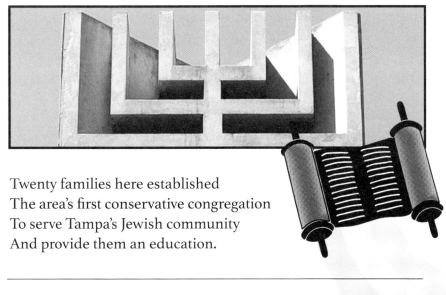

Twenty families here established
The area's first conservative congregation
To serve Tampa's Jewish community
And provide them an education.

Along a beloved boulevard
Never falls, but rises this Wave—
The road to the city's investment in art
Did this acquisition help pave.

_____

_____

10

Today the American Legion
Holds fast to its founding mission.
Outside its Tampa outpost you'll find
A submarine's ammunition.

_____

_____

11

A symbol of transformation
You'll find in a garden well-known.
Inside of a red brick circle,
It spreads its wings of stone.

12

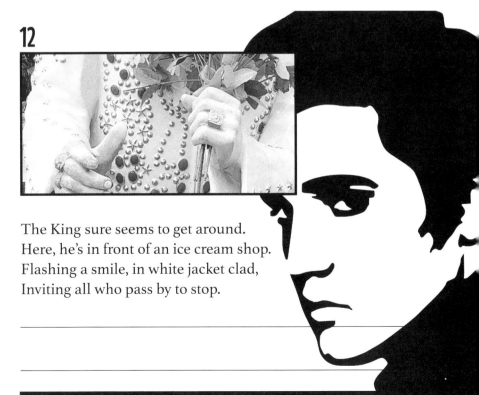

The King sure seems to get around.
Here, he's in front of an ice cream shop.
Flashing a smile, in white jacket clad,
Inviting all who pass by to stop.

13

From gastropub to restaurant group,
Local foodies have watched it grow.
They've opened up a bakery, too—
Now they're rolling in the Dough.

14

One of the trees at this corner
Is not like those that surround it.
It has a bit more personality—
Take a picture once you've found it.

15

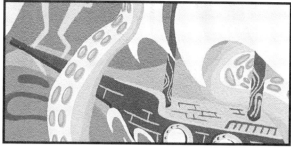

A skeletal pirate has claimed this wall,
In his hand he wields a sword,
While in the distance a Kraken attacks
A ship and those aboard.

16

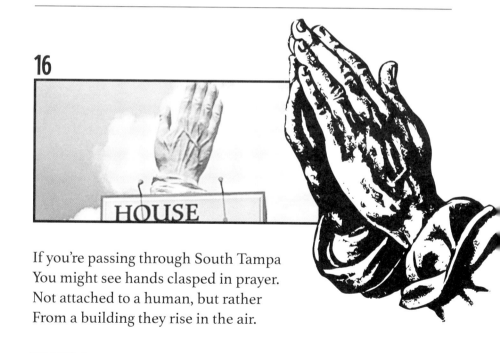

If you're passing through South Tampa
You might see hands clasped in prayer.
Not attached to a human, but rather
From a building they rise in the air.

1

No sign now marks this structure
That was used in the Civil War.
You'll find it toward the end of the park
Where it once produced salt by the shore.

_____

_____

2

An eagle keeps watch atop this post
Which remembrance's road once marked.
A hundred and five, the cost in lives
From Hillsborough they embarked.

_____

_____

3

If you like drinking Mai-Tais
To the sound of a ukulele,
Ben T. Davis leads the way
To a place you can do so daily.

_____

_____

4

Atop this particular building
Seems a rather odd place
For aliens to park their craft
On their travels from outer space.

_____

_____

5

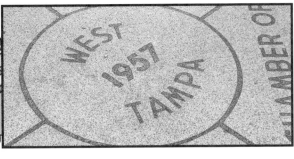

First beneath Hugh's arches pass
Then up the hill, a structure to find.
A circle in the center gives the time and place
'Round which four civic groups combine.

6

A well-known sports team owner,
For 37 years The Boss,
Stands now in bronze before the field
Where big apple and big guava cross.

7

Follow the Road to Recovery
Until the tall sails appear.
Words of wisdom along the way
Help many to overcome fear.

_____

_____

8

The original record-holder
For the most balls caught in a game—
Today you can find his likeness
In the park that bears his name.

_____

_____

9

Look up at the spherical object
Perched on a slender tower.
Often do its owners brag
Of its prognostic power.

10

Some editorials need no words:
Holding up a child without tiring.
This fez-adorned symbol of healing and hope
So many have found inspiring.

11

The first field in this neighborhood
(From which it takes its name),
This marker explains was for aircraft,
Not for playing a football game.

12

1718

The first and oldest in the county,
Built from donated Carnegie dollars,
For over a century the public has served
From novice readers to scholars.

1

Later her name became Pocahontas;
Legends of her kindness survive.
When she dared to intervene
And spare a Spaniard from roasting alive.

2

If you find that you're not in Kansas,
Then to Tampa Heights you should go.
There, you'll encounter this crew on a quest
Along the Yellow Brick Row.

3

Near this marker camped two units,
Buffalo Soldiers, proudly named;
Black infantrymen that overseas
Medals of Honor for valor claimed.

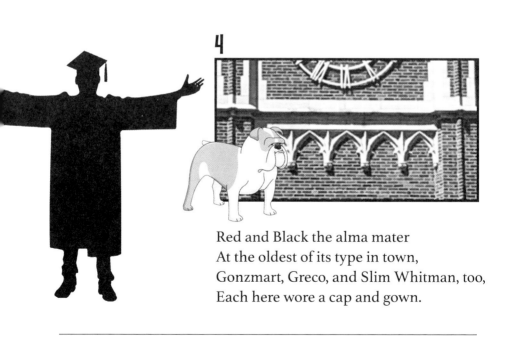

4

Red and Black the alma mater
At the oldest of its type in town,
Gonzmart, Greco, and Slim Whitman, too,
Each here wore a cap and gown.

5

One of the Fairyland figures is poised
High atop the restaurant wall.
Perhaps the staff or the princess nearby
Will reassemble him, should he fall.

6

Inside an old warehouse reborn
This cephalopod chooses to lurk,
Perched on a beam above the heads
Of sushi chefs at work.

7

This innovative beer-mobile
Gave a local business its name.
They've since expanded from offering tours
And have achieved as a brewery acclaim.

_____

_____

8

Once known as the Michigan Avenue Bridge
With rare bobtail swing designed,
One of its features, a bridge tender's house,
To obsolescence has now been consigned.

_____

_____

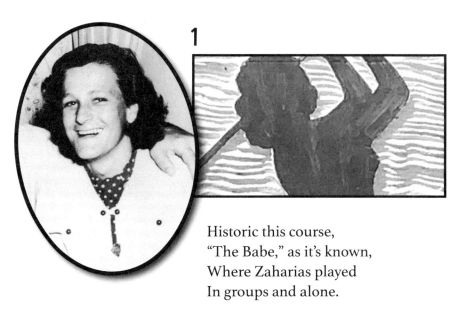

1

Historic this course,
"The Babe," as it's known,
Where Zaharias played
In groups and alone.

2

Outside of a local home goods store
An unexpected spectacle:
Made to carry a picnic lunch
For giants, this receptacle.

3

A long time under construction,
It's not a new mall or hotel.
It's the home of a prominent businessman,
A doctor and donor as well.

4

This sculpture tells a tale of love
Between two spheres in space.
Though only seldom they share the sky,
In this work of art they embrace.

5

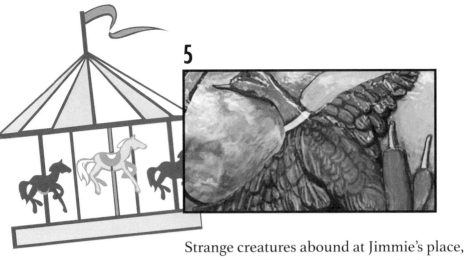

Strange creatures abound at Jimmie's place,
These several are getting strange looks.
It seems they've escaped their carousel;
Now they're circling children's books.

_____

_____

6

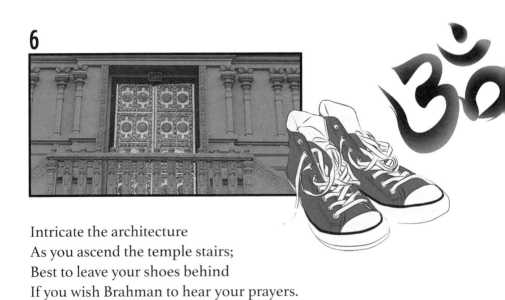

Intricate the architecture
As you ascend the temple stairs;
Best to leave your shoes behind
If you wish Brahman to hear your prayers.

_____

_____

7

Sawmill owner Lutz connected
Odessa to Tampa by rail.
The old wooden trestle bridge you seek
Can be found on the Upper Trail.

8

Horses, dragons, and a panda, too—
Around in circles they spin.
The mall today they call their home
Though Venice their origin.

1

They say two heads are better than one,
And my dual visages took me far,
From the egg in the nest from which I hatched
To a place on display at the bar.

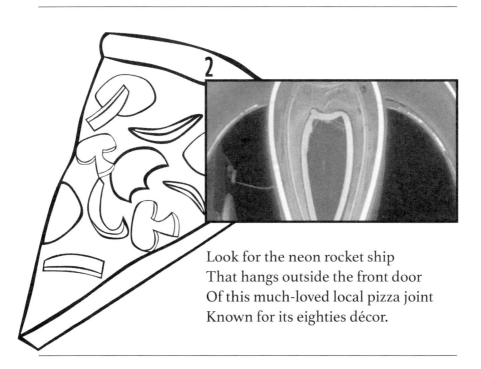

2

Look for the neon rocket ship
That hangs outside the front door
Of this much-loved local pizza joint
Known for its eighties décor.

3

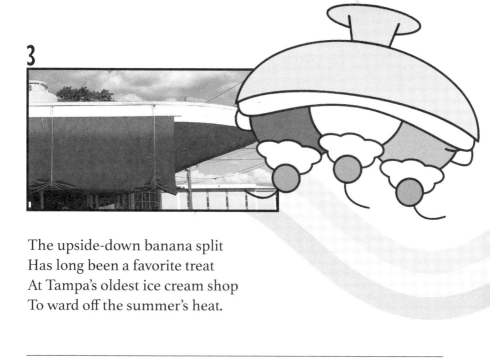

The upside-down banana split
Has long been a favorite treat
At Tampa's oldest ice cream shop
To ward off the summer's heat.

4

Once lived in this farmhouse a captain,
His parents the first townfolk to wed;
With a mantle, perhaps, from the Hiram Cool,
Under which the hearth he fed.

5

In front of a place for beer and wine
Stands a colorful, two-headed reptile.
He does not wear a coat of scales,
But rather mosaic tile.

6

This mural has some good advice
All seekers should take to heart.
To paraphrase its message here:
"It matters not where you start."

7

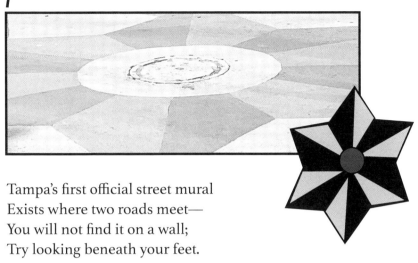

Tampa's first official street mural
Exists where two roads meet—
You will not find it on a wall;
Try looking beneath your feet.

8

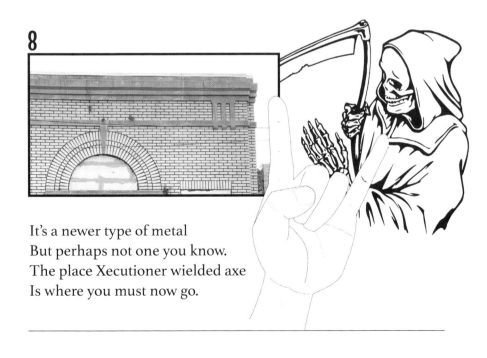

It's a newer type of metal
But perhaps not one you know.
The place Xecutioner wielded axe
Is where you must now go.

9

In 1863, not far away,
Burned the ships of James McKay.
Both blue and grey, the dead that day—
The sole such skirmish at Tampa Bay.

10

Why it stands now where it does
So very few can say.
Was it a fort that was put there for sport?
Or a lighthouse that lost its way?

11

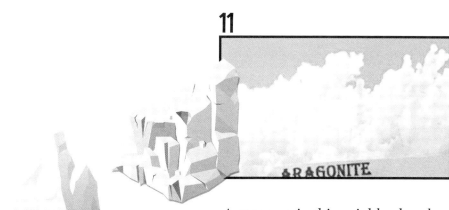

A museum in this neighborhood
Named for pungent springs run dry
Keeps a display of rocks and stones
You're sure to find if you try.

_____

_____

12

Forming memorable natural connections
Is the mission of this place,
Where species under protection can roam
More than 50 acres of space.

_____

_____

1

A beer baron built a garden,
The people to entertain.
But you must be this tall to soar and to fall
On the rides that they maintain.

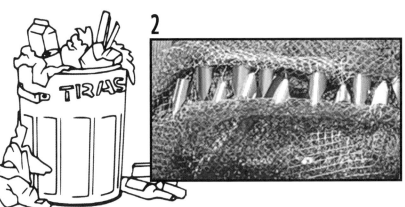

2

This giant red garbage guardian,
The museum, its home, it protects.
Prehistoric its form may be,
But industry its content reflects.

3

Eight tendrils rotate from the center
And connect to the ground below.
On specific dates and times each year,
The sun sets key points aglow.

Fig: 1.

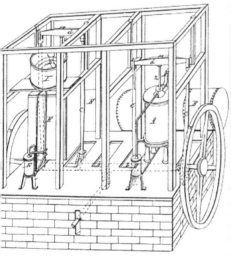

4

Alongside his fellow inventors,
John's face you'll find on the wall.
Of all the ideas in Florida made real
His was the coolest of all.

5

Three bulls in bronze you'll find here,
Charging up a storm.
Not unlike some credit cards
Of freshmen in the dorm.

6

This artwork snakes up a building wall,
Two thousand disks there pinned.
Reflecting light off their surface like water
And changing with the wind.

7

There, in his eponymous plaza,
Today a King does gleam,
Not the one with blue suede shoes,
But the one who had a dream.

8

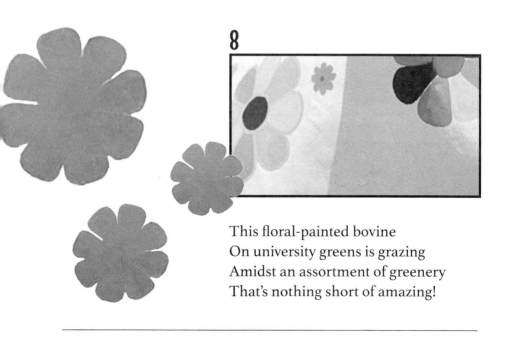

This floral-painted bovine
On university greens is grazing
Amidst an assortment of greenery
That's nothing short of amazing!

1

If you're on the way to Plant City
You'll see plenty of stores and shops.
But at only one place among them
Will you find a triceratops.

_____

_____

2

When Jim Crow was the law of the land
Hotels were not open to all on vacation.
Instead, at Janie's house, they'd inquire
To find accommodations.

_____

_____

3

From woven strands emerge a scene:
Plants here rooted will never wilt.
Preserved behind glass, three panels across.
In the lobby, admire Josette's quilt.

4

A celebrated berry on Cherry you'll find
Filled with water from the tower.
It may look tasty, but don't even try,
For this one you cannot devour.

5

The town of Ichepucksassa
You won't find on a map today.
Renamed, but still its heart you seek,
On a brick wall fading away.

6

King Louie's face, half-painted blue
Might make a passerby stop,
At least that's Frank and Wenda's hope
In planting this royal outside their shop.

7

The transport of lumber and phosphate
Helped the city to grow and thrive.
Step back in time, when aboard you climb
Seaboard Air Line 5735.

8

With wings outspread at the library,
This avian statue looks regal.
It has, however, some students confused,
As their mascot's a hawk, not an eagle.

Pinellas County

Just west of Hillsborough, Pinellas County includes the cities of St. Petersburg, which is known for its arts and culture scene, and Clearwater, which is recognized for its beautiful beaches. The county features an extraordinary diversity of activities and history, from the shell mounds of indigenous people to the landing site of conquistadores, historic beachfront hotels, internationally acclaimed museums, and winning local sports teams such as the Rays and the Rowdies.

1

Demen's named one city
For another which gave him the boot.
Find a place where the twain may meet
And a friendship has taken root.

2

IN COMMEMORATION OF THE
WORLD RECORD
FOR 10 MILES
45 Minutes 37 Seconds

Set At This Location By

Ondoro Osoro
of KENYA

For running 10 miles an hour
No track coach would give you flack.
But cut that time by a quarter
And you'd have earned yourself this plaque.

3

NEW YORK METS
ST. LOUIS CARDINALS

The Mets bring back former star pitcher

From this spot the street was once plated;
Baseball history fans were elated.
Then came construction, some plates faced destruction.
To elsewhere they've been relocated.

4

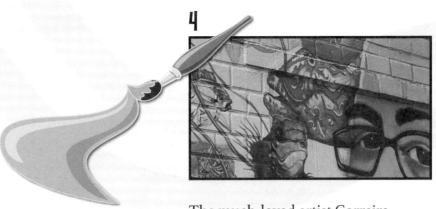

The much-loved artist Correira,
Better known to some as Woo,
Is the subject of this mural, by which
The community pays him his due.

5

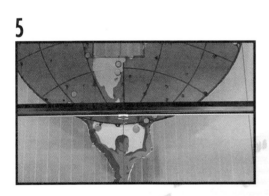

"Stack it high and sell it cheap,"
Doc Webb was a clever feller.
Find the remnants of the city he built
In a brewery-adjacent cellar.

6

This famous sixties supermodel
Has stars fixed in her eyes,
Fittingly made to be larger than life
In this artwork by Chad Mize.

_____

_____

7

Enter through the canyon
To the city's old southwest;
There, inside the Jewel Box, find
What Misses love the best.

_____

_____

8

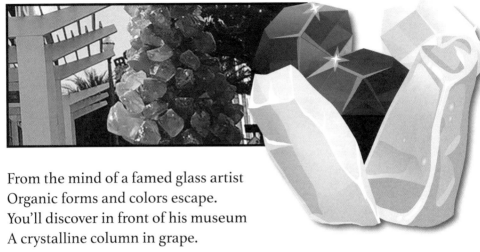

From the mind of a famed glass artist
Organic forms and colors escape.
You'll discover in front of his museum
A crystalline column in grape.

9

In spite of everything,
I still believe that
people are really good
at heart.

—ANNE FRANK

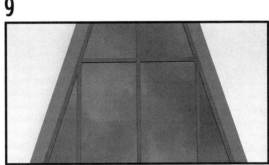

The victims of a genocide
Here speak through the artifacts.
If you find you're moved to share your thoughts,
Slip a message into the cracks.

10

Many ice cream shops in the Burg
Now infuse with booze what they vend
But this one was among the first
To launch the tasty trend.

11

If you're seeking surrealist artwork,
Here you'll find an incomparable cache.
Wander behind the oddly shaped building
And there find the artist's mustache.

12

There's a treasure behind the museum:
A spiral of purest gold.
Artists and architects know it well,
And the Greeks from days of old.

13

A Health City gimmick this fountain,
Dispensing more water than truth—
It comes from a plain old municipal tap
And will not restore your youth.

14

To a bump in the road all quests must come,
But seldom that bump gets a name.
This one's a landmark and local cheap thrill,
Worth passing over just once, some claim.

_____

_____

15

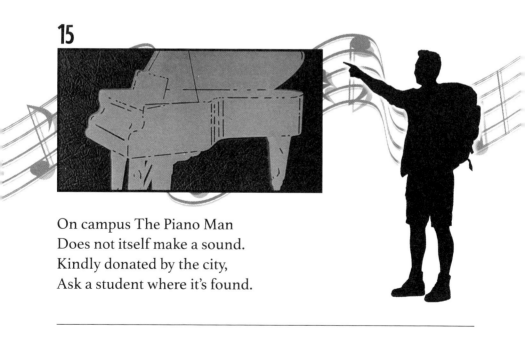

On campus The Piano Man
Does not itself make a sound.
Kindly donated by the city,
Ask a student where it's found.

_____

_____

1

Where concrete transcends water
You can peer into the past
In the form of the former pilings
Of a pier that did not last.

2

Silently hawking papers
Is this boy's eternal task—
On days that see no sunshine
Not a cent from you he'll ask.

3

She came to town by way of boat,
As she might have once traveled the Nile.
She's ancient but not indigenous,
Though she's resided here for a long while.

4

What one man collects, others use for play,
An object designed to be cast away.
Penned between the stitches is what turns them to riches
And makes them truly worthy of display.

5

Me, again!

On the very first day of 1914,
If you looked up from the statue at this site,
Perhaps the Benoist you might have seen
On its short but historic, very first flight.

6

This miniature St. Mary's
Has provided to many relief,
Save for the spirit that's trapped inside
(If in ghosts you have a belief).

7

Inside this Romanian wine bar,
Flights of white and red to be had,
The décor might strike some as batty
With its obvious homage to Vlad.

8

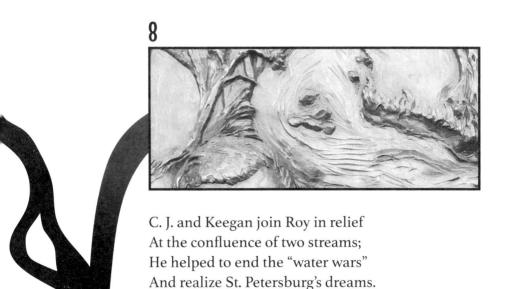

C. J. and Keegan join Roy in relief
At the confluence of two streams;
He helped to end the "water wars"
And realize St. Petersburg's dreams.

9

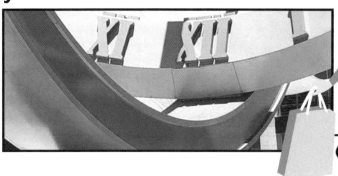

To learn from this piece the time of day
So many seldom stop.
Though it gives them the power to know the hour,
It mostly invites them to shop.

10

Innovation and government buildings,
Some say, seldom go hand-in-hand.
This open-air structure bucks that trend
As the first of its kind in the land.

11

In the center of the city's first park
You'll find William Harvard's shell.
Around its angular canopy,
Locals gather sometimes for a spell.

12

This brick, neoclassical princess
Has hosted athletes and presidents.
In her rococo-styled rooms,
Seniors are now her residents.

13

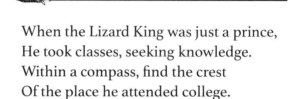

When the Lizard King was just a prince,
He took classes, seeking knowledge.
Within a compass, find the crest
Of the place he attended college.

_____

_____

14

A sport once popular with retirees,
Now en vogue with a younger crowd,
At the largest of such clubs in the world:
The public on Fridays are allowed.

_____

_____

15

Twelve red chairs here planted,
All different in shape and size.
The diversity of county juries is
What the installation implies.

16

From ancient to modern inhabitants,
This isn't some mirage;
Six different cultures that shaped this land
Grace the wall of a parking garage.

1

From the drained lake that became a garden
Comes a legend of which few know—
A stone upon which those who sit
Are able to make plants grow.

_____

_____

2

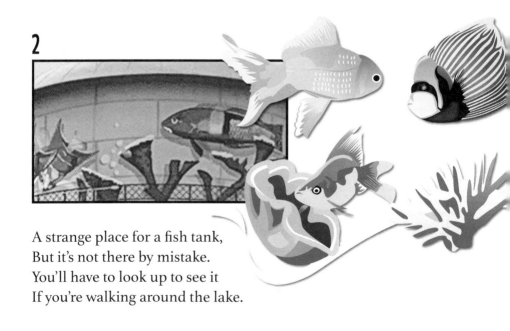

A strange place for a fish tank,
But it's not there by mistake.
You'll have to look up to see it
If you're walking around the lake.

_____

_____

3

Papa must be in trouble again:
He's always picking fights.
Maybe that's why he's at this law firm
Seeking help in defending his rights.

4

This sign isn't going anywhere,
It's fixed with a ball and chain.
The notion that it might run off,
Well, quite frankly, that's insane.

5

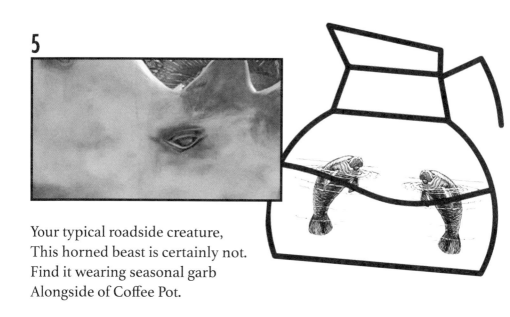

Your typical roadside creature,
This horned beast is certainly not.
Find it wearing seasonal garb
Alongside of Coffee Pot.

6

This vintage 1920s hotel
Taylor made for Mister Laughner
Once more draws guests from near and far,
Perhaps even from the hereafter.

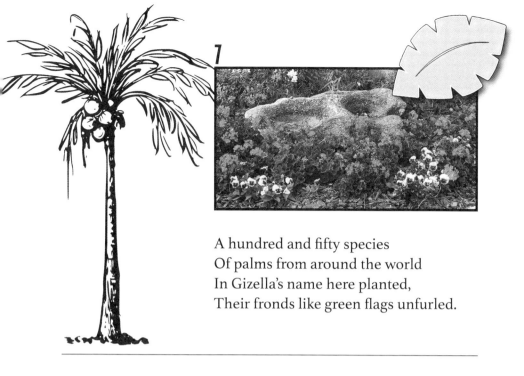

7

A hundred and fifty species
Of palms from around the world
In Gizella's name here planted,
Their fronds like green flags unfurled.

8

Many in number the churches and temples
Where worshippers offer devotion,
But there is only one such place
For those who seek harmony in motion.

1

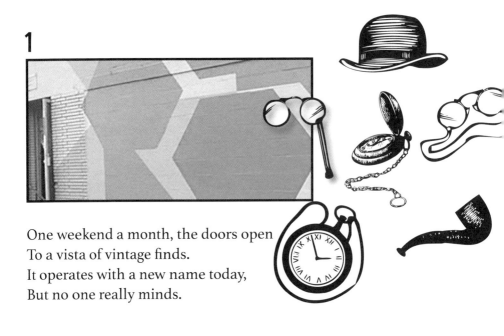

One weekend a month, the doors open
To a vista of vintage finds.
It operates with a new name today,
But no one really minds.

2

If I were to brew the world,
I'd include a secret place:
A bibliophile's throne room
Hidden behind a bookcase.

3

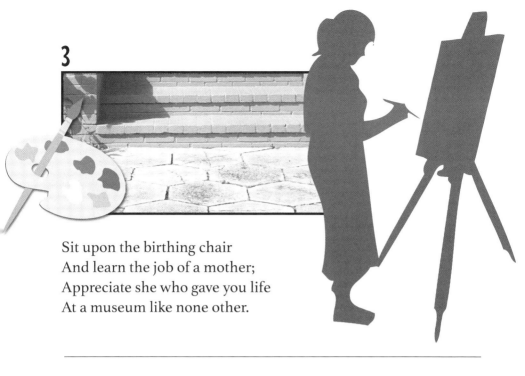

Sit upon the birthing chair
And learn the job of a mother;
Appreciate she who gave you life
At a museum like none other.

_____

_____

4

There beside the old train depot,
Where sculpted portal stands ajar,
Find fragments of the Berlin Wall
In the lot where you park your car.

_____

_____

5

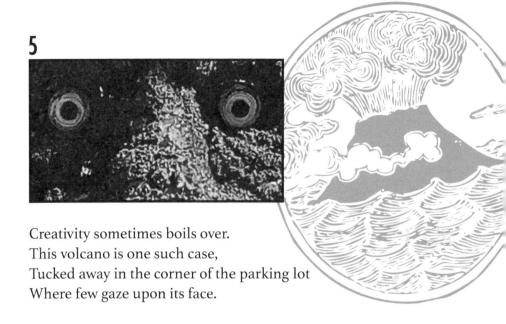

Creativity sometimes boils over.
This volcano is one such case,
Tucked away in the corner of the parking lot
Where few gaze upon its face.

6

Two lions guard the temple,
Its threshold you can't cross, of course,
As it's just an elaborate illusion,
Here conjured by the artist Palehorse.

7

This geometric artwork
Is a maze of mirrors and light.
Through the portal, if you gaze—
You'll find no end in sight.

8

Alice, the Hatter and the Cheshire Cat,
On the side of this building you'll spy.
But it's the rabbit you're looking for:
Surely, he must be nearby.

9

A legend from Hollywood's golden age
Brings to town glamour and grace.
Three muralist brothers have captured here
A beauty that time can't erase.

10

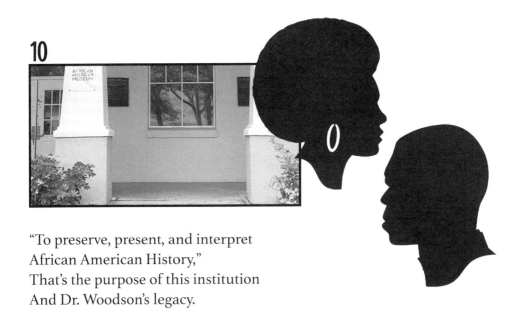

"To preserve, present, and interpret
African American History,"
That's the purpose of this institution
And Dr. Woodson's legacy.

11

From slavery to business owner—
A path he could not have planned.
By the casino find his likeness,
Standing there with his hat in hand.

12

The African American Heritage Trail
Illuminates this housing's mission
To provide the growing population
With a better living condition.

1

Morris made the casino his home,
His "mansion by the sea."
Though he can't go inside it, you'll find him beside it
For all of eternity.

2

On one knee this robot's poised
Along the garden trail,
With a bouquet of flowers he passes the hours;
Will large, muted blood-pump prevail?

3

At the Gibbs campus
You'll find this sight,
Metal artwork that spins,
Refracting light.

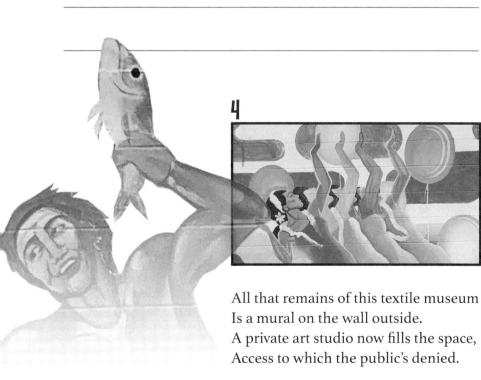

4

All that remains of this textile museum
Is a mural on the wall outside.
A private art studio now fills the space,
Access to which the public's denied.

5

A fortune in hats
Its namesake made,
At this place where attorneys
Learn their trade.

_____

_____

6

JUNGLE PR

THIS PROJECT WAS
FLORIDA DEPARTME
THE FLORIDA RECREA

Legends are told of the men seeking gold;
From Spain it was they departed.
But they found here no gain, only bloodshed and pain,
From the place exploration started.

_____

_____

7

No druidic monuments,
Despite this small park's name.
Capture the mermaid waiting there
In a photo as proof that you came.

8

The Jungle Country Club Hotel
Was a place to stay on vacation.
Nowadays, it's a boarding school
And first step to a future vocation.

1

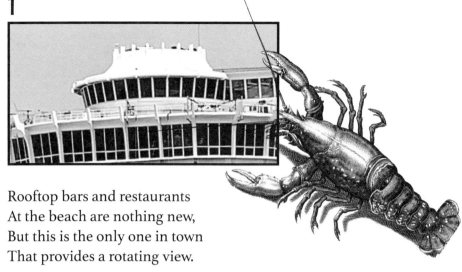

Rooftop bars and restaurants
At the beach are nothing new,
But this is the only one in town
That provides a rotating view.

2

"The Tiki," this Easter Island Moai is called,
Its glowing green eyes clearly seen.
You'll find it near a coiled serpent
At a quirky putting green.

3

Mister Rowe was a fellow to know—
The king of his own sandcastle.
It's pretty in pink, a nice place for a drink,
But owning the thing was a hassle.

4

The sea creatures on the gallery wall
Are there to make visitors smile.
They frolic around a pink sandcastle
All made of mosaic tile.

5

From the ocean and beach
To the other end of town,
You can hear this bell ring
Each day at sundown.

_____

_____

6

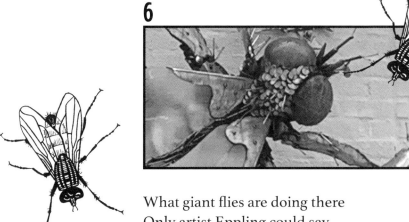

What giant flies are doing there
Only artist Eppling could say,
But that's where you'll find them, face to face
On the side of the alleyway.

_____

_____

7

This marker reveals that the Spaniards
Here kept a fishing camp.
Sometime later, Zephania
Upon it put his stamp.

8

In the early 1900s,
On this dock Joseph built his store.
Hubbard's name once graced the pier
But now it's Merry once more.

1

The Kahuna of Tiki Gardens
Here rests his gargantuan head.
No longer the god of a theme park,
He's now an exhibit instead.

2

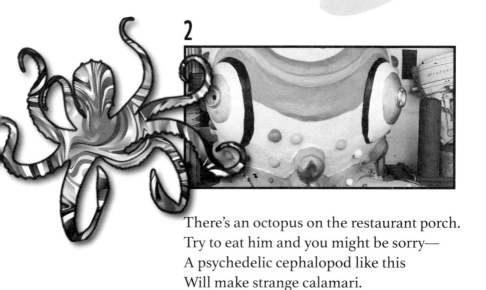

There's an octopus on the restaurant porch.
Try to eat him and you might be sorry—
A psychedelic cephalopod like this
Will make strange calamari.

3

The theme park known as Tiki Gardens
Is now forever out of reach.
Its name, however, can still be found,
Granting access to the beach.

4

Sussor provided the fishermen bait,
But they wanted booze and a snack,
So he decided to charge them for drinks
From his infamous, glorified shack.

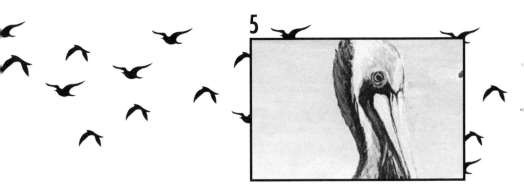

5

Here find many feathered friends
In need of a wing and a prayer,
Some to the wild will be released
After having medical care.

6

Bucky stands atop a chest,
Raising his saber high.
No one, it seems, has informed him
That the treasure was always a lie.

7

Near the community center and park
Is a place a musician might rest—
It sports a famous composer's name
As well as a musical crest.

_____

_____

8

To walk along such a white sand beach
Many folks spend their whole lives dreaming.
And once each year, sculptors gather here,
Turning grains into artworks gleaming.

_____

_____

9

A popular place to browse the aisles
For nautical crafts and supplies,
The Old Florida shopping experience
That awaits you will no doubt surprise.

10

Formed in 2011,
To orphaned animals here they cater.
No longer a refuge for reptiles alone,
But still you can kiss a gator.

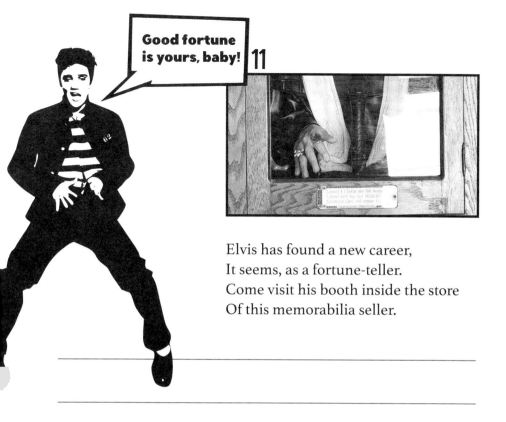

Elvis has found a new career,
It seems, as a fortune-teller.
Come visit his booth inside the store
Of this memorabilia seller.

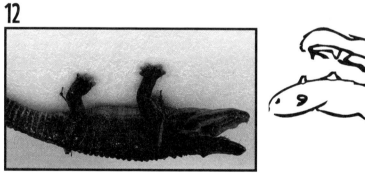

Walking along John's Pass,
You might get an uneasy feeling;
Perhaps it's the gator overhead
That's walking on the ceiling.

13

This shark is a fish out of water
And a photogenic spoof,
Crashing through the restaurant
And coming out of the roof.

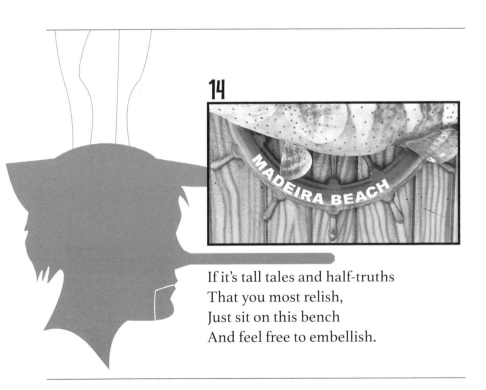

14

If it's tall tales and half-truths
That you most relish,
Just sit on this bench
And feel free to embellish.

15

Fishermen know every cast of the line
Is both a prayer and a bet;
Take a moment here to recall
Those caught in Poseidon's own net.

16

Many flock to see this church
And its unintended feature:
That its Spanish-style tower
Resembles a barnyard creature.

1

Visit now the oldest log cabin
In the county of Pinellas.
It stands among peers, preserved through the years
With the stories such structures can tell us.

2

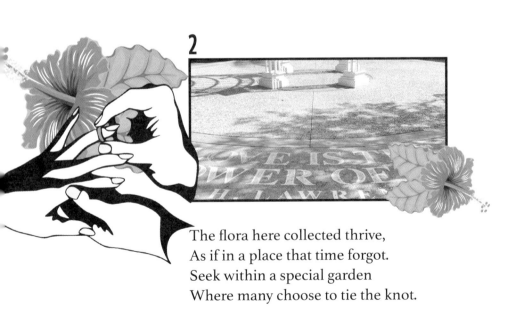

The flora here collected thrive,
As if in a place that time forgot.
Seek within a special garden
Where many choose to tie the knot.

3

It only runs on the weekend,
And only 12 weekends each year.
Its sole stop is Largo, with children its cargo;
When it passes you by, give a cheer.

_____

_____

4

This store was built to serve the needs
Of those who put food on your menu.
Moved to the park, it's now a museum
And small-to mid-sized venue.

_____

_____

5

To some, the body's a canvas—
Their tools are needles and ink.
This gallery collection of their trade makes art:
Observe it and see what you think.

_____

_____

6

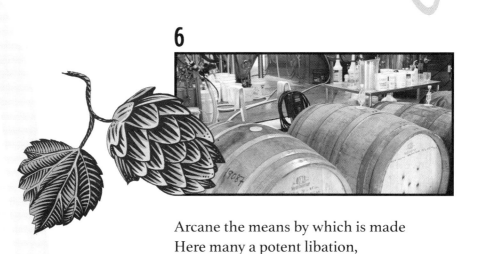

Arcane the means by which is made
Here many a potent libation,
As malt and hops and yeast achieve
Both sweet and sour sublimation.

_____

_____

7

Five branches meet in this small park,
Though none attached to a tree.
A winged sentry waits at the nexus,
Prepared to defend liberty.

_____

_____

8

Many a president, celebrity, and mogul
Have been the White Queen's guest.
She was rescued from the wrecking ball
When JMC chose to invest.

_____

_____

1

From kapok seed a wonder sprouted
Into a strange garden of stone.
Though the restaurant in its day was loved,
It closed down for reasons unknown.

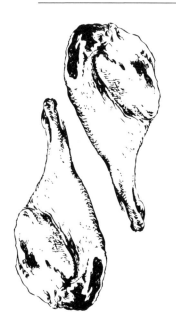

2

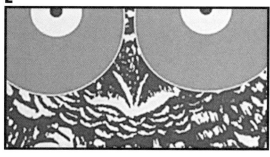

When six partners this venture launched,
Most thought they were insane.
With a tacky double entendre,
On this spot was born a chain.

3

Metal fish, a petri dish,
Decorative bones of whale,
A prosthetic limb, if that's your whim;
All can be found here for sale.

4

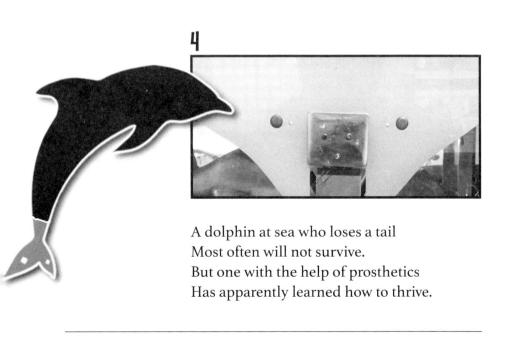

A dolphin at sea who loses a tail
Most often will not survive.
But one with the help of prosthetics
Has apparently learned how to thrive.

5

This statue by the water honors
The area's very first Greek.
On Narvaez's doomed expedition
It was gold, not sponges, he'd seek.

_____

_____

6

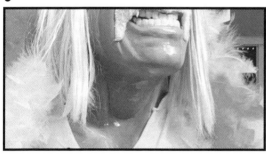

This famous sidewalk likeness,
Known for ripping apart his shirt.
In earlier days a wrestling star,
Later the subject of tabloid dirt.

_____

_____

7

The tower turns from blue to grey
Each morning as darkness dissipates.
Behind the design is Thomas Sign,
A century it commemorates.

8

By the marina standing
Back to back, these manmade shells.
Do they pine for the water nearby
Whenever the flood tide swells?

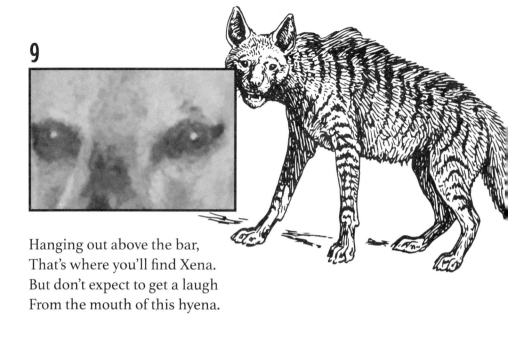

9

Hanging out above the bar,
That's where you'll find Xena.
But don't expect to get a laugh
From the mouth of this hyena.

_____

_____

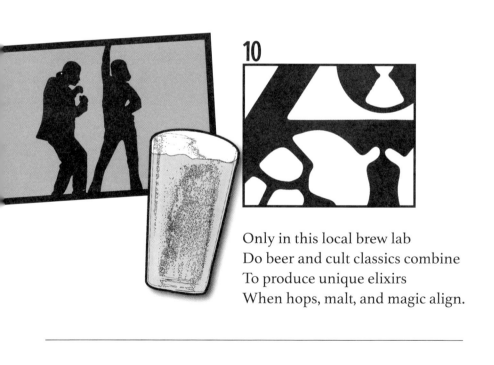

10

Only in this local brew lab
Do beer and cult classics combine
To produce unique elixirs
When hops, malt, and magic align.

_____

_____

11

This torch of metal ladders
Is impossible to douse;
You'll find the public sculpture
Outside the firehouse.

_____

_____

12

No schoolbooks here
Or students in class,
This building now houses
Clearwater's past.

_____

_____

13

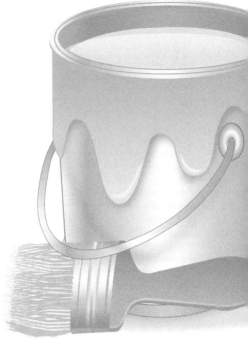

This home was once the paint store
Of Ralph and Florence Plum—
When vacated by their grandkids,
Dr. Nach bought it for a fair sum.

14

One thousand and eighty feet long it stretches,
A popular place to give sunset a look.
Lined with vendors and fishermen
Seeking tarpon, trout, and mackerel to hook.

15

This group of three is all you will see
Of the famous Dolphin Trail.
The rest of the painted porpoises
At the park have all turned tail.

16

This panel of honor for 90 years hidden,
Revealed during renovation,
Lists names of the locals who valiantly served,
All worthy of our veneration.

This oak outside the library
Didn't grow from another tree's seed.
With its sunset-colored foliage,
It will not ever water need.

18

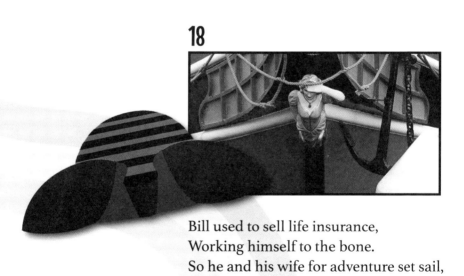

Bill used to sell life insurance,
Working himself to the bone.
So he and his wife for adventure set sail,
As Captain Memo he's known.

19

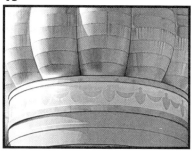

To reach Bagdad,
You needn't travel long,
Its towers to a
Senior community belong.

20

When a blessed image on windows appeared,
Some declared it to be a sign.
Though headless now, Mary's shoulders still
Are preserved at this office-turned-shrine.

1

It's magic when lovers realize
That they fit like lock and key.
What better way to share their joy
Than affixing the former to me?

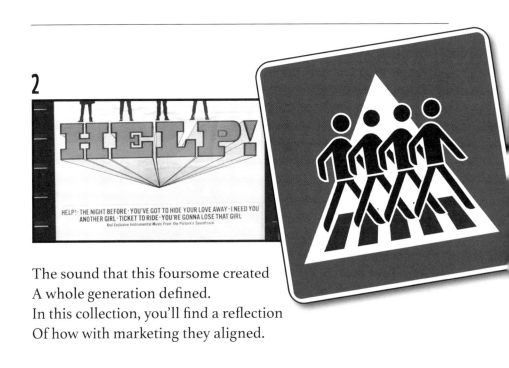

2

The sound that this foursome created
A whole generation defined.
In this collection, you'll find a reflection
Of how with marketing they aligned.

3

This sweet tribute to a local mayor
In mint condition will remain:
Proof that his taste as a business owner
And "angel investor" was not in vain.

4

The first such center in the US
For an ancient form of exercise,
Here, next door to an old hotel,
Can one become graceful and wise.

5

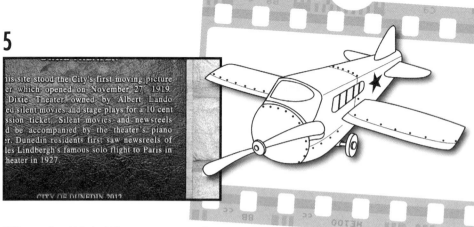

is site stood the City's first moving picture
er which opened on November 27, 1919.
Dixie Theater owned by Albert Lando
ed silent movies and stage plays for a 10 cent
ssion ticket. Silent movies and newsreels
d be accompanied by the theater's piano
r. Dunedin residents first saw newsreels of
les Lindbergh's famous solo flight to Paris in
heater in 1927.

CITY OF DUNEDIN 2012

When the Dixie Theater opened,
A dime was the price of a night.
Here you could catch a silent film
Or newsreel of Lindbergh's flight.

_____

_____

6

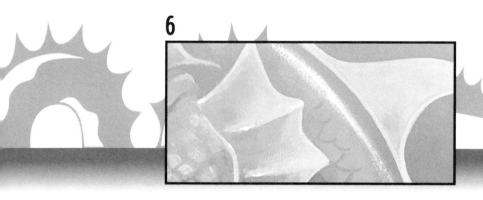

Many in search of sea serpents sail
But only ever catch pneumonia.
All the while, there's one that wants to be seen
On the wall of Caledonia.

_____

_____

7

Observe the home of Dr. Willis,
Who built here his "nature nook."
From his perch in a tree he wrote down what he'd see
When over the bay he would look.

_____

_____

8

Here find kegs and metal tanks
Which Scottish flair adorn.
Florida's oldest microbrewery
In 1995 was born.

_____

_____

1

In this collection of rare machines
With bells, chimes, and flashing light,
You'll find restored the games you adored
And once fed with tokens all night.

_____

_____

2

This former stop on the Orange Belt
Now preserves relics of days gone by.
In one of its nooks you'll find children's books
By the author of *Jack Horner's Pie*.

_____

_____

3

The first of the town's sponge divers
Lie here in eternal repose.
Find them and pay your respects
Behind the gates of Rose.

4

This neighborhood mother's green thumb
Tended her garden and rooted out weeds.
Today not a tree but a mosaic mural
Remembers her kind and good deeds.

5

G.I. Joe, Barbie and Matchbox cars
Here await nostalgia's demand—
A refuge from adulthood for some;
Safe place for cubs in a grizzly land.

6

This tower no longer casts a beam
For sailors at night on the seas.
Atop a tripod this riddle awaits;
Unlock it with Anclote's Keys.

7

The doctor amassed a collection of art
By Picasso and his own stepdad.
To be the recipient of such a gift,
The college was only too glad.

8

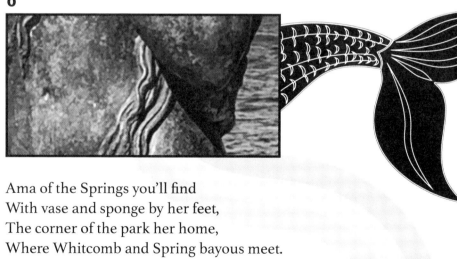

Ama of the Springs you'll find
With vase and sponge by her feet,
The corner of the park her home,
Where Whitcomb and Spring bayous meet.

9

Two men helped build an industry,
John Cheyney and John Cocoris.
One diver on their docks forever endeavors
To retrieve for them treasure most porous.

10

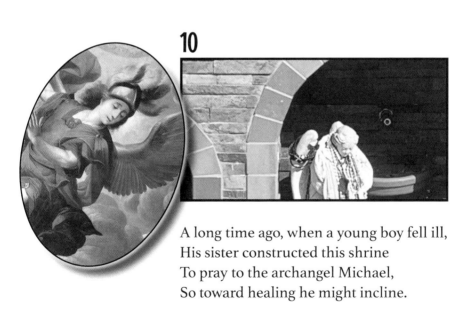

A long time ago, when a young boy fell ill,
His sister constructed this shrine
To pray to the archangel Michael,
So toward healing he might incline.

11

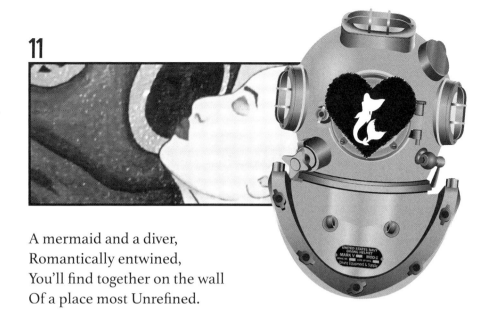

A mermaid and a diver,
Romantically entwined,
You'll find together on the wall
Of a place most Unrefined.

12

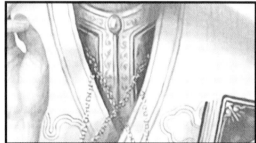

When Nicholas started weeping,
No one could figure out why—
Which isn't surprising, after all,
Most paintings of saints don't cry.

1

Your short human span means nothing at all
To an elderly giant like me.
Since I was a sprout, I've had never a doubt
That the harbor will afford me safety.

_____

_____

2

In the park and on the stone
That bear this Frenchman's name,
You'll divine how tobacco and grapefruit
Earned him enduring fame.

_____

_____

3

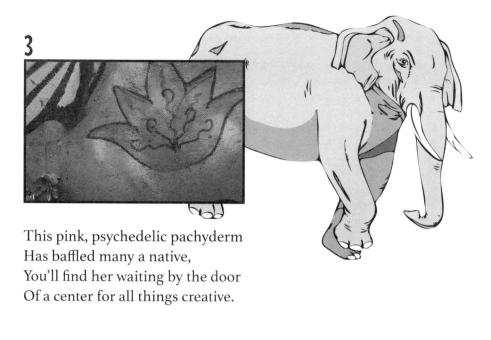

This pink, psychedelic pachyderm
Has baffled many a native,
You'll find her waiting by the door
Of a center for all things creative.

4

For over 200 years sprouted
This oak from a sacred shell mound.
The shells were removed and used as road base,
But the tree itself remains sound.

5

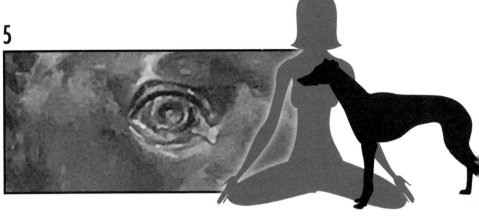

Zeus guards the site of healing springs,
Or so thought one physician;
Today it's the lobby of a hotel spa
Where this sentinel holds his position.

6

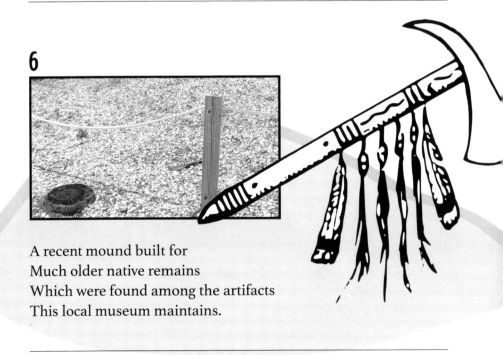

A recent mound built for
Much older native remains
Which were found among the artifacts
This local museum maintains.

7

These cows outside the old station
Are more colorful than their ilk,
Creative and painted with strange designs:
I'm not sure I'd drink their milk.

8

This mural atop the station shows
First responders from days gone by.
Mules and horses speed them along;
To get there in time, they'll no doubt try.

9

He's the R. E. O. in the speedwagon,
The same are his name and mobile.
His monument in the eponymous park
Stands tribute to this big wheel.

_____

_____

10

From two pillars of oxidized gears,
This pair of metal wings spread
Outside of what once was the local bank,
Where history's kept now, instead.

_____

_____

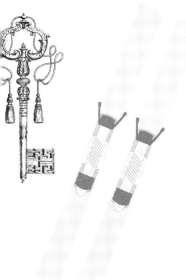

11

"The Mightiest in the South," they claim,
As far as such markets go,
From antique keys to used water skis,
What you'll find there, you just never know.

12

Trying to find a more scenic path,
some say will come to no avail,
Visit now this community park
And walk along the Eagle Trail.

1

Some folks inherit a family home,
Antiques, or maybe a car,
But a sanctuary for primates,
Well, that is much stranger, by far.

2

Many the local orchards and farms,
But only one Rockford Peach.
You won't find her on the pitcher's mound
Or sunning herself at the beach.

3

It can be a deadly encounter
If by a copperhead one's bit.
But you've nothing to fear from the one stationed here,
Guarding the course's snake pit.

4

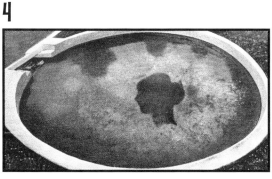

In this pool some think they see
A woman's silhouette,
But those who dive in to save her
Will find that they only get wet.

Manatee and Sarasota Counties

Established in 1855, Manatee County originally encompassed Sarasota and includes the city of Bradenton, as well as the suspected landing site of Hernando De Soto. Starting around 1883, The Florida Mortgage and Investment Company of Edinburgh began acquiring land in Sarasota. These early Scottish settlers played a key role in developing the area. John and Mabel Ringling, Bertha Potter Palmer, and many others helped transform Sarasota into a gleaming cultural gem along the Gulf Coast.

1

It only stands to reason
That if the road has rules,
Then those who are sworn to enforce them
Must learn them all in schools.

2

Three Keys you must find
This riddle to solve.
Don't let the libations
Erode your resolve.

_____

_____

3

This town took its name from the castle
When founding brothers found only trouble.
After disasters and hassle, abandoned;
Ringed now by mobile homes its rubble.

_____

_____

4

Skills and spears ancient hunters kept sharp
To strike when the moment was right.
Find within a museum display
This example of early man's plight.

_____

_____

5

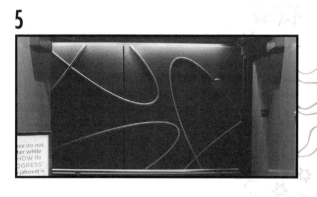

It's science, not faith, this Bishop preserves:
Flora and fauna in specimen jars.
Find here a dome under which to observe
The movement of planets and stars.

_____

_____

6

Pirates you'll find in the Magic River,
But not of the pillaging sort;
Rather, a team with a stadium here,
In the spring, where they practice their sport.

7

This marker tells the story
Of Robert's Dollar Limit stores.
Even though the name has changed,
His business today still endures.

8

Pre-Columbian mounds here stood
Where the Currys arrived from Key West.
Before that, a place of refuge and peace
Where freed slaves would not be oppressed.

9

Two parabolic dishes
Poised to harness reverberation:
Both artwork and acoustic space,
Fertile ground for contemplation.

10

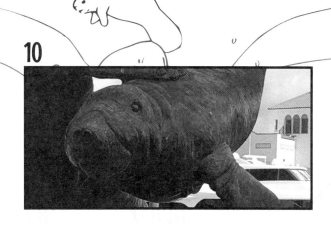

By the water's edge you'll see these two,
Perhaps a parent and child.
While sea cows are not so uncommon,
This particular pair you won't find in the wild.

11

A biker, a golfer, a shuffleboard player
Wave to each other morning, night, and noon
From the tiles of this mosaic in which
They invite you to come back soon.

1

Across the sea this explorer was sent
As the Spanish crown demanded.
On this spot in 1539
He and his crew first landed.

2

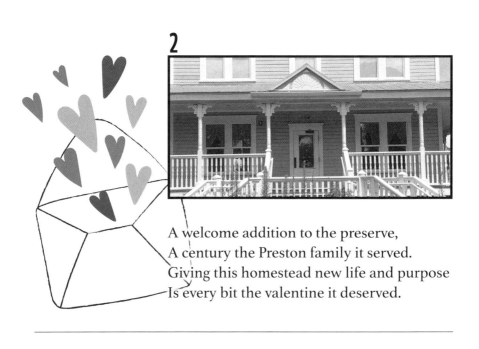

A welcome addition to the preserve,
A century the Preston family it served.
Giving this homestead new life and purpose
Is every bit the valentine it deserved.

3

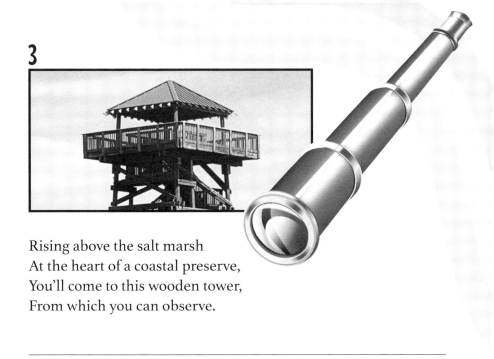

Rising above the salt marsh
At the heart of a coastal preserve,
You'll come to this wooden tower,
From which you can observe.

_____

_____

4

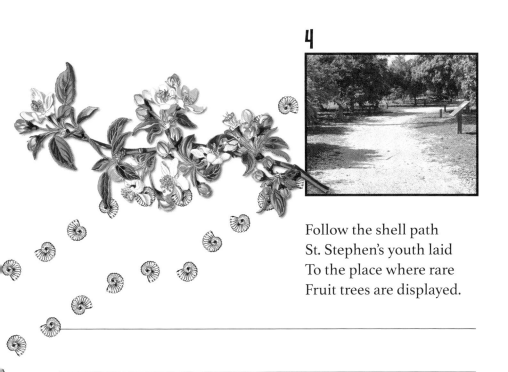

Follow the shell path
St. Stephen's youth laid
To the place where rare
Fruit trees are displayed.

_____

_____

5

Deanna Belle would weather hell
To bring her catch ashore.
You might be shocked she's now landlocked,
Where she casts her nets no more.

6

Inside this old brick schoolhouse
A fishing village's past
With models and tools for building ships
From stern to prow to mast.

7

From icehouse to automotive garage
And sea turtle hatchery,
Now this building serves as home
To the island's history.

8

Over the water it stretches,
This pier more loved than its peers,
Though frequently it's been assailed by storms
For more than a hundred years.

9

8:18 PM

Every evening at this beach restaurant
With your server you can place a bet
Then wait for the bell and the winner's announced:
Who guessed closest the time the sun set.

_____

_____

10

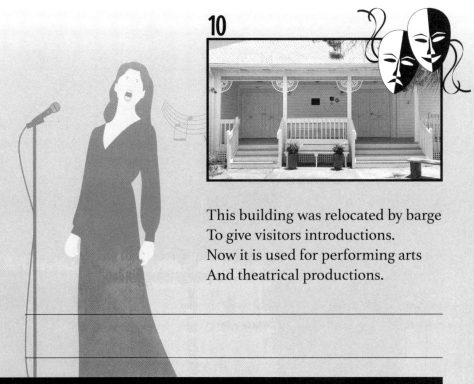

This building was relocated by barge
To give visitors introductions.
Now it is used for performing arts
And theatrical productions.

This grouper is known for its ugliness;
It won't make a tasty meal,
Composed as it is of unnatural bits
Of welded scrap metal and steel.

If you cast your coins and wishes here,
You might feel a bit like a fool.
It isn't a well, but it once housed the bell
From the island's previous school.

1

Colonial, Greek, and Italian Renaissance,
Styles to this unique structure amount.
Built by a prominent citrus grower,
Later the home of a Russian Count.

2

"The House of John"
Is this home's name—
Tribute to his vision
And circus fame.

3

Upon this historic Italian stage,
The actress Duse was known to play.
Acquired and shipped piece by piece overseas,
Reassembled where it stands today.

4

Not the knight from King Arthur's court
But the rarest of circus attractions,
Lancelot in this tapestry hides
Among the myriad visual distractions.

5

This mansion an inventor built
As a winter home for his wife
With the fortune he made selling auto parts
When direct mail changed his life.

6

Since the 1930s,
Generations recall with warm smiles
Watching the birds here ride their bikes
And getting up close with reptiles.

7

Collected here are classics,
Like Ringling's Silver Ghost.
The second-oldest such museum
In the country is its boast.

_____

_____

8

The last show Abe attended
Was certainly his worst,
Shortly thereafter, his final ride
Was in this type of hearse.

_____

_____

9

A snowman there along the gulf,
Now, isn't that whimsical fun!
Thankfully, though, this one won't melt,
No matter how hot the sun.

_____

_____

10

The fort once known as Juan Ortiz
Long ago met its end.
Its last outpost, now lonely, stands
With nothing left to defend.

_____

_____

11

Something has surfaced from the deep
Outside of a center for art,
Clad in brightly painted scales—
It must be creative at heart.

12

This auditorium fountain
Was moved when its style no longer fit,
To the Ringling and then into storage before
Returned to its rightful place and relit.

1

In this controversial statue
Some see victory at first glance,
But what one considers a harmless embrace
Is to others an unwanted advance.

2

Captured at this fountain
You'll find four dolphins at play.
The bayfront forms the backdrop
While they're leaping though the spray.

3

To work in Marie's banyan grove
Many a horticulturalist yearns—
It's the only such place for display and study
Of epiphytic orchids and ferns.

4

This sandstone pillar capital
Honors the city's first hundred years.
From Glasgow, like those who nearby landed,
Seeking their fortune and new frontiers.

5

In the center of one loop,
Another stands suspended.
Differences inextricably bound
Is perhaps what the artist intended.

6

From premodern Japanese warrior
Comes this artwork's inspiration.
Curved like a blade, of aluminum made;
Find it beside the bus station.

7

This neoclassical skyscraper,
Its original appearance retains.
From bank to hotel to senior home,
Still the Orange Blossom remains.

8

The city's first skyscraper,
Though it only has seven floors,
From stable to ice house and pool hall,
As executive suites it endures.

9

A message you'll find at
This flagpole's base laid
For buddies (meaning veterans),
Here thrown a parade.

10

At the corner in front of the theater
Is where this Fey lady sings.
She could fly anytime from her pedestal
With a flap of her butterfly wings.

11

Kat and Herman, Helen and Joe
Took their act to new heights, crossing wires.
Come and remember them at this plaque
Whenever your heart desires.

12

Over a dozen patriots here
Are not divided by nation or party,
Where busts of American presidents
Are joined by Artigas and Marti.

13

Once a teenage runaway
Before learning to captain a yacht.
Seek out his nautical-themed abodes,
Where many a course did he plot.

_____

_____

14

JomaR

To have breakfast on Circus Saturdays
The curious gather from near and far
At this relic, museum, and restaurant on wheels,
To some, better known as JomaR.

_____

_____

15

The Scotsman who introduced golf to the gulf
Was here the first mayor elected.
Seek you now his resting place
Where many have genuflected.

16

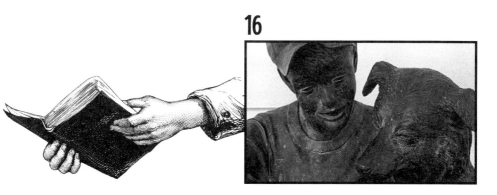

This boy and his companion
On the bench are taking a rest
And reading together from a book—
That's friendship at its best.

17

Fairy tales and fantasy
Brought to life in this garden park.
When you find three pigs in front of their homes,
Take a picture, just for a lark.

_____

_____

18

Near the old railway depot
Is a symbol the city knows well:
Observe in the form of a sculpture
This gargantuan metal seashell.

_____

_____

19

This classical revival, wood-frame home
Was moved from Euclid Avenue
To a place more befitting of pioneers,
Thereby giving Alfred and Mary their due.

20

Often the circus performing arts
Call to mind death-defying thrills,
But those who attend this academy
Also acquire more practical skills.

1

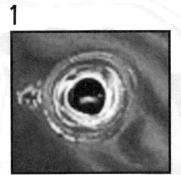

Molly's no monster and hardly a threat,
Preserved behind glass in a tank.
Forever now passive with eyes that are massive,
She stares, unseeing and blank.

2

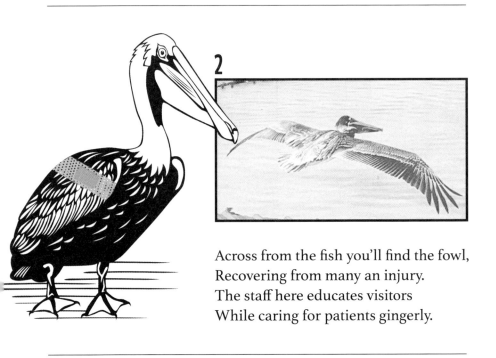

Across from the fish you'll find the fowl,
Recovering from many an injury.
The staff here educates visitors
While caring for patients gingerly.

3

You can walk and kayak through tunnels
Formed from branches of mangrove tree
Just a short distance from downtown,
Yet worlds away on this beachgoers' key.

4

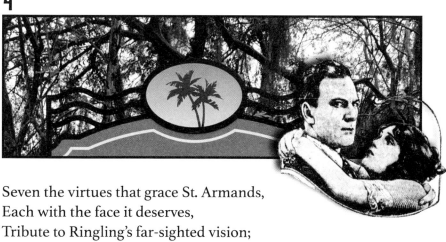

Seven the virtues that grace St. Armands,
Each with the face it deserves,
Tribute to Ringling's far-sighted vision;
Michelangelo approvingly observes.

5

In St. Armands Circle
Search not in the stores,
If that which you're seeking
Is the tiniest of doors.

6

Most think of this name
For Hawaiian shirts.
Who knew they served dinner,
Mixed drinks and desserts.

7

All throughout Sarasota
Ringling's legend is undiminished,
Not even by the restaurant that stands today
Where his hotel was never finished.

8

To end segregation at the beach,
This mural recalls, some would not rest.
So they organized weekly wade-ins
Until victorious in their quest.